Treasury of Stories

Created by
Don and Chris Wise

Illustrated by
Kelly R. Pulley
Danny Brooks Dalby

Special thanks to:
John Jordan, Lisa Reed, Randy White, Dan Hosse, Sandy Hosse,
Patricia Thompson, Cindy Helms, Shannon Doyle

Published by
Louis Weber, C.E.O.
Publications International, Ltd.
7373 North Cicero Avenue
Lincolnwood, Illinois 60646

Don Wise, Producer
Debbie H. Bush, Vice President of Publishing
Performance Unlimited, Inc.
1710 General George Patton Drive, Suite 110
Brentwood, Tennessee 37027

Permission is never granted for commercial purposes.

Manufactured in the U.S.A.

8 7 6 5 4 3 2 1

ISBN: 0-7853-2115-2

J 220.95
BEG

Stories from the Old Testament

Stories from the New Testament

Stories from
the Old Testament

Creation

Genesis 1–2

Before there was anything, there was God. God created heaven and earth. God saw that the whole earth was dark and empty. He also saw that darkness covered everything. He said, "Let there be light." God called the light "day" and the darkness "night." This was the first day.

On the second day God created a great big space where he put blue skies and fluffy white clouds. God saw all these things, and they were good! This was the end of the second day.

On the third day God made a place for all the oceans, rivers, and seas. He made the dry lands appear. On the dry lands God made many kinds of bushes, trees, flowers, and plants. There were beautiful plants growing everywhere. All these things pleased God. This ended the third day.

On the fourth day God said, "Let there be bright lights all over the sky." In the day the sun would light up the earth. The warm rays from the sun would help the plants grow. At night a moon would shine. Then God created twinkling stars and spread them all over the night sky. God made all things, and he saw that it was very good. And that was the end of the fourth day.

When the fifth day came there was more God wanted to do. On this day God filled the waters with all kinds of things. There he made big blue whales and brightly colored shells, and many different colors of fish. Then God said, "Let every kind of bird fill the sky and fly high above the earth." And God saw that what he created was good.

On the sixth day God filled the dry land with all kinds of wonderful animals. There were cute furry animals and scaly ones, too. Some could move fast, and some were very slow. God saw that all these things were good.

God said, "I will make a man named Adam. He can rule over the fish, birds, and animals." So God made the first human. God saw that it was all very good. On the seventh day God saw that all his work was done, and he rested. God blessed this day and made it holy.

Adam was the first man God created. God made a very special garden in Eden where Adam could live. Adam was given a big job. His job was to work the land and take care of the garden. God also told Adam he could eat from any tree in the garden except one. The one he was not to eat from was the tree of knowledge of good and evil. God also brought all the animals to Adam so he could name them. Whatever Adam called the animals that would be their very own special name.

Even though Adam was surrounded by beautiful plants, trees, and animals, something was missing. Adam felt very lonely. God already knew Adam was lonely.

"It is not right for you to be alone," said God. So God made another human. Her name was Eve. Now Adam and Eve would live together in the beautiful Garden of Eden.

Adam and Eve

Genesis 2–3

Adam and Eve lived in the most perfect place in all the world. It was filled with many beautiful flowers and trees. God gave Adam and Eve fresh water to drink and plenty of food to eat. God only gave them one rule to follow. There was a tree that grew in the middle of the garden. God told Adam and Eve, "You may eat the fruit from any tree in the garden except this one."

One day Eve went for a walk. She wanted to pick some fruit. She was very surprised when a tricky serpent said to her, "Is it true? Did God really tell you not to eat from that one tree over there?"

Eve told the serpent what God had said to them. Then the serpent replied, "But this fruit will make you wise like God. Look how pretty it is. Do not worry about what God said. Go ahead. Take one and try a bite. It's really good."

Eve agreed that it did look tasty. So she picked the fruit from the tree and took a bite. After Eve ate some, she gave some to Adam. They both ate the fruit from the tree even though they knew God said it was wrong.

God was walking through the garden that night. Adam and Eve tried to hide. They were afraid because they knew they had broken the one rule God had given them. But no one can hide from God.

"Where are you?" asked God.

"We are over here," said Adam. "We were afraid."

"Why are you hiding?" asked God.

Adam and Eve had to tell God that they had disobeyed the one rule they had been given. Adam said, "Eve gave me fruit from the forbidden tree, and I ate it."

Then God asked Eve, "What have you done?"

Eve replied, "The serpent tricked me and said that the fruit would make us wise like you."

Even though they said these things to God, they knew they had done wrong. God said to the serpent, "For the rest of your days, you will have to crawl on your belly."

Then God spoke to Adam and Eve. He said, "You have done a terrible thing. You disobeyed me. Now you can no longer stay in the garden."

So Adam and Eve left the beautiful garden. Then God sent an angel with a flaming sword to guard the entrance. No one would ever be allowed into the garden again.

Noah and the Ark

Genesis 6–8

After Adam and Eve lived in the Garden of Eden the world began to change. Now many people lived on the earth. But the people became evil. They did not follow God. This made God very sad. God looked all over the earth to see if anyone was still good.

He was happy when he found a man named Noah. God had a special plan for Noah and his family. God told Noah, "I am going to wash away all the evil in the world with a great flood. I will make the world new again."

First God told Noah to build a special boat, called an ark. God explained to Noah what an ark was and exactly how to build it. This boat was very important for God's plan. Noah listened carefully. It was important that he do everything exactly as God said.

The ark was going to be very, very big. God told Noah to build the ark three stories high. Noah was instructed to put a roof on the ark and a wide door in the side.

God also told Noah to build the ark out of gopher wood and paint it with a thick glue that would make the ark waterproof. Now it would not leak.

People laughed when they saw Noah building a really big boat so far away from water. Everyone thought Noah was silly. But Noah trusted God. He built the ark just as he was told. He did not let the people bother him.

"The ark is finished! What should I do now, God?" asked Noah.

God told Noah, "You are to put two of every kind of animal on the ark."

Noah thought to himself, "Where will I find all of these animals?" Then a great thing happened.

God sent every kind of animal to Noah. They came to him two by two. Noah followed God's plan exactly, and he made sure all the animals were safe inside the ark.

But there was still much more work to be done. Next God said to Noah, "Gather lots of food for your family and the animals to eat. You must store it inside the ark."

Noah did just as God said and loaded the ark with all kinds of fruits and grains. There would be plenty of food for everyone.

Now that the animals and food were on the ark as God had asked, it was time for Noah and his family to get on board. After they were all safe inside God said, "I am going to make it rain."

Big clouds covered the earth. The sky began to darken. Lightning flashed across the sky. Rain began to fall from the sky. Water began to cover the ground.

Soon there was so much rain that even mountaintops disappeared. And just as God planned, all the earth was covered with water! But God protected Noah, his family, and the animals. They were all safe from the storm. Noah and his family took care of each other and the animals, too.

For 40 days and 40 nights, God made the heavens rain down upon the earth. Then one day, just as quickly as it had started, the rain stopped. Noah peeked out of a window. He wanted to know what everything looked like. He also wanted to see if there was any land around. So he sent a beautiful black raven in search of dry land. The raven flew far away. But it could not find any land or even a tree to rest on, so it flew back to the ark.

Noah waited a week and then sent out a dove. Before long, the dove came back with a surprise! It returned with an olive branch. The dove had found dry land! This was Noah's sign that the water was finally going down.

Once again, Noah decided to send out the dove. When the dove did not return, Noah knew what it meant. It was almost time to leave the ark.

The ark finally stopped floating. It came to rest on top of a big mountain. Noah opened the door and looked out. The land was new. The air was fresh. Then all the animals came out of the ark. Everyone was so happy to be back on dry land. The first thing Noah and his family did was build a special altar. They all gave thanks and praise to God for keeping them safe.

Then God placed a rainbow across the sky. No one had ever seen a rainbow before. It was a wonderful sight. God said, "This will be a sign of my promise to all of you. I will never again cover the whole earth with water. From this day on, whenever you look up at the sky and see my rainbow, remember this promise I have made to you, your family, and all mankind."

Abraham and Sarah

Genesis 12–21

Abraham and Sarah believed and trusted in God. One day, God said to Abraham, "Leave your home, and I will guide you to a new land. In that new land I will bless you and your family." So Abraham and Sarah packed up their belongings and made the long journey to the new land. Abraham's nephew, Lot, traveled with them.

God guided them to the new land of Canaan. Abraham's helpers and Lot's helpers began to argue. Abraham said, "Choose the land you want and go live there." Lot picked the best land for himself. Abraham and Sarah moved their tents to the big trees at Hebron.

One hot afternoon, Abraham saw three men coming toward his tent. He called out to them, "Welcome, visitors. Come. Rest and eat by my tent."

Abraham ran inside the tent and said, "Sarah, we have visitors." Right away Sarah began to bake bread for them to eat. Abraham brought cool milk for them to drink.

When the food was ready, Abraham and the three men rested under a tree next to the tent. "Where is your wife?" the visitors asked.

Abraham told them, "My wife is inside the tent."

Then one of the visitors said something unusual, "Soon, Sarah will have a baby boy." Sarah was listening inside the tent. When she heard what they said, she laughed to herself. She knew she was too old to have a baby. She was over 90 years old. Why would this stranger say such a thing?

The visitor spoke again. He asked Sarah, "Why did you laugh? Is there anything that God cannot do?"

Sarah was embarrassed. She had not meant for anyone to hear her. She was afraid and said, "I did not laugh."

But the visitor said, "Yes, you did."

When Abraham heard the visitor say these things, he knew that it was God speaking to them. And before the year was over, Sarah had a baby boy. She remembered how she had laughed when God told her that they would have a baby.

Everyone was surprised that God had given Sarah a child. Abraham and Sarah were very happy. In fact they were so happy they named the baby boy Isaac, which means laughter. They also remembered to thank God for their very special blessing.

Joseph and His Brothers

Genesis 37–46

There was a man named Jacob who had a very large family. He had 12 sons. Jacob loved all his sons, but he loved Joseph most of all. His other sons were jealous of Joseph because of all the attention their father gave him.

One day Jacob gave Joseph a very special coat. It was decorated with many beautiful colors. Jacob said, "Look at this nice coat I got for Joseph." Joseph loved his coat of many colors. He made sure everyone got to see it.

Joseph put on his coat and said, "I am very happy! Father loves me so much he gave me this wonderful coat." But this made Joseph's older brothers even more jealous.

One night, while Joseph was sleeping, he had a dream. In the dream he and his brothers were gathering stalks of grain. Suddenly Joseph's grain stood up. Then the grain his brothers were gathering bowed to Joseph's grain. When Joseph told his family about his dream, his brothers glared at him. Angrily they asked, "Who do you think you are that we would bow down to you?"

Soon after this happened, Joseph had another dream. This time he dreamt that the sun, the moon, and 11 stars bowed down to him. When Joseph told his brothers about this dream, they were very angry. They wondered if Joseph might try to rule over them. They did not want Joseph to tell them what to do. When Joseph told his father about the dream, Jacob asked, "Does this dream mean that your mother and I will bow down to you, too?"

JOSEPH AND HIS BROTHERS

One day Joseph visited his brothers as they tended the sheep in the fields. When the brothers saw Joseph, they grabbed him and threw him in a dry well. Then they sold Joseph to some traders for 20 pieces of silver. The traders took Joseph far away to Egypt. When Joseph did not return home that night with his brothers, their father was so sad he cried. He thought Joseph was dead.

Even though Joseph had done nothing wrong, he was put into jail. But God did not forget about him. He gave him the ability to understand the meaning of dreams. Some of the king's workers were in jail, too. When they had dreams, they came to Joseph. Joseph would tell them what their dreams meant. One night the king had a dream. He had heard that Joseph could tell him what his dreams meant. So the king called for Joseph.

Joseph stood before the king. He listened to the king tell about his dreams. In one dream the king stood by the river. First seven fat cows came out from the river. Next seven thin cows came out of the water and stood by the fat cows. Then the thin cows swallowed the fat cows. In another dream the king saw seven ripe ears of corn growing next to seven dried-up ears of corn. The dried-up ears of corn ate the ripe ears.

Joseph told the king, "God is telling you about things that are going to happen. The seven fat cows and seven ripe ears of corn mean that there will be seven years when plenty of food will grow. The seven thin cows and seven dried-up ears of corn mean there will be seven years of famine when nothing will grow. Egypt will have seven years to get ready for the time when nothing will grow."

Joseph told the king to save the extra grain during the first seven years when good crops grew. The extra grain would be stored for use during the seven years of famine. The king said, "This is a very good plan." So the king put Joseph in charge of the palace and all the kingdom so he could make these things happen.

After the seven growing years, the time came when no food would grow. The famine spread far and wide. People from all over the world came to Egypt. They would have to ask Joseph if they could buy food.

One day Jacob sent his sons to Egypt to buy food. The brothers did not know their brother Joseph lived in Egypt. They did not know what an important person he was in the kingdom. When Joseph's brothers arrived, they did not recognize him. Joseph pretended not to know them.

Joseph thought of a way to make his brothers return to Egypt. He accused them of being spies. "We are not spies," they said. "Our father sent us to buy food."

Joseph said, "Prove to me that you are telling the truth. Leave one brother in Egypt. Then the rest of you can take the grain and go home. When you return for more grain, you must bring your youngest brother to me."

Soon the brothers had to return to Egypt to buy more food. They kept their promise and brought their youngest brother with them. When Joseph saw everyone, he almost cried! He said, "I am Joseph, your brother. How is our father?" The brothers were afraid. But Joseph said, "Do not worry. God made these things happen so that I would be able to save Egypt." They celebrated, and Joseph's family moved to Egypt so they would all be together again.

Moses

Exodus 1–15

After Joseph there was a new king. He was afraid of God's people. He thought they might try to take over his kingdom. The king made God's people work hard so they would be tired. One day the king shouted, "I do not like these people. Throw their baby boys into the river."

One mother planned to save her baby. She hid him in a basket and floated it in the river. She told the baby's sister to watch over him. The king's daughter found the baby. She wanted to keep him. The baby's sister asked, "Do you need help with the baby?" When the princess said yes, the baby's sister brought her own mother to help.

The baby's mother took good care of him. She taught him many things. When it came time, she took the child to live in the palace with the princess. The princess named the baby Moses.

As Moses grew up, he had many nice things. He had good books to read, good food to eat, and nice clothes to wear. But even with all these things, he was still unhappy living in the palace. Moses did not like the way the king treated God's people. The king made them work very hard and was mean to them. Moses wanted to move away from the mean king. He decided to leave the palace. So one day Moses left everything behind in Egypt. He traveled far away to become a shepherd.

Once while Moses was watching the sheep, he saw a burning bush. The bush did not burn up even though it was on fire! God spoke to Moses through the burning bush. He said, "Moses, I want you to go back to Egypt. You must tell the king to let my people go." Moses wanted to obey God, but he was afraid. God said, "Do not be afraid, Moses. I will be with you."

But Moses was still afraid. He asked God, "What if the king does not listen to me?"

So God said to Moses, "Throw your staff onto the ground." When Moses did this, the staff turned into a snake. Then God told him to pick it up again. Moses did what God told him. The snake turned back into a staff. God said, "I will use signs like this to show the king that I am with you." Moses trusted God and went to Egypt.

He went to see the king. "Let God's people go," he said. But the king was very stubborn. He refused to obey God's command. Moses wanted to show the king that God was with him. God sent many plagues upon the land. He made all of the water in the land turn into blood. No one could drink it, and even the fish could not live in the water. But the king would not let God's people go. So God sent frogs, and then he turned the dust on the ground into pesky gnats.

The king said, "I will not let the people go."

God sent flies to Egypt for the next plague. The king sent for Moses. He said, "Your God is much too powerful. Take your people and go away." The king also told Moses to take the flies away. But when Moses took the flies away, the king changed his mind. He made God's people stay.

Next God made the Egyptians and their animals sick. The king would still not let God's people go. So God made hail fall on the ground. It ruined all of the Egyptians' food. The king said, "Enough! Take your people and go." But as soon as the hail stopped, the king changed his mind.

God was determined to show his power. For the next plague, locusts were sent to eat all the fruit on the trees. The king said, "Take away all the pests, and then you may go." But the king did not keep his word. Even after God made complete darkness fall over the land for three whole days and nights, the king would not let God's people leave.

God said, "The oldest boy child in each Egyptian family will die. The others will be safe." These things happened just as God said. Finally the king called for Moses and said, "Take God's people and go."

God's people left Egypt quickly. God helped them find their way through the desert. He led them with a cloud by day and a pillar of fire by night. After they had traveled for many miles, God's people arrived at the Red Sea. By this time, the king had changed his mind again. He sent his army to bring them back. Now God's people were trapped between the Red Sea and the king's army. Moses reminded God's people, "Do not worry. God is with us."

God took care of them. He sent a big wind. It made a dry path right through the middle of the sea. God's people walked on the path and safely over to the other side.

The king's army tried to follow them through the sea, but God protected his people. He closed the water back over the army. God's people were happy to finally be free and safe. They sang songs of praise to God.

Joshua

Joshua 1–6

Moses had been the leader of God's people for a long, long time. Now it was time for a new leader. Joshua was God's choice. He would be the one to lead God's people into the promised land.

God's people were camped just outside Canaan. Joshua knew they needed to conquer Jericho before they could live in Canaan. Joshua also knew God would help them. Joshua sent two spies to Jericho. He wanted them to bring him news about the city and the people who lived there.

The two spies went into Jericho. They knew they must be very careful. If anyone found out they were there, they would be in great danger! They hid in the house that belonged to a woman named Rahab. But the spies did not know that someone had seen them sneak into the house. That person ran to tell the king about them.

Right away the king sent soldiers to Rahab's house. The soldiers told her to send out the spies. Rahab was a very quick thinker. She said, "There were two men here, but I did not know who they were. They left before the gate around the city was closed for the night. I do not know where they went. But if you hurry you might catch them." The soldiers looked in her house, then went away.

Rahab had hidden the spies on her roof. She ran up to them after the soldiers left the house and said, "We have heard of all the wonders your God has done. Since I have protected you from the king, will you promise to protect me and my family when you attack the city of Jericho?"

The spies made a promise to Rahab. When they came to take over the city, they would make sure she was safe. She would gather her family together inside her home. As a signal to show where they were, Rahab would tie a red rope to the window. The spies went down a rope and went back to the safety of their camp. Then they told Joshua that the people of Jericho were afraid of them and their God. Joshua knew this was good news.

Before God's people could enter the land of Canaan, they had to cross the river Jordan. Joshua knew they needed to trust God. He listened very carefully as God told him how to get the people across the river. Early the next morning God's people packed up their camp. They brought out the Ark of the Covenant, a very special golden chest that held the laws of God. The priests carried the Ark.

When they arrived at the river Jordan, the priests who were carrying the Ark of the Covenant went first. As they stepped into the river, its waters parted. There was a dry place for God's people to walk on to get to the other side. As the leaders crossed the river, each one chose one stone from the middle of the river. Then they stacked them on the other side. Whenever they would look at the stones, they would remember how God helped them.

As soon as everyone reached the other side, the river began to flow again. When they were close to Jericho, Joshua looked up and saw someone standing in front of him. He asked, "Are you for or against us?"

The person said, "Neither. I am for God's army." Joshua knew this was an angel from God. He listened carefully to the angel. The angel told him exactly how to fight the battle to take over the city of Jericho. Joshua's army was to march around the wall one time every day for six days. Seven priests would march in front of the army carrying trumpets. They would carry the Ark so everyone would know that God was with them. On the seventh day, they were to march around the wall six times. On the seventh time around, the priests were to blow their trumpets and the entire army was to shout loudly.

Joshua did all these things just as God had told him. God's people circled the wall surrounding Jericho. The Ark and the priests with trumpets led the way. They marched around the wall once each day for six days.

On the seventh day, they marched around seven times. When they started their seventh trip around Jericho's wall, Joshua gave the signal. The priests began to blow mightily on the trumpets. All the soldiers began to shout. The city's wall began to tremble, shake, and crumble. Then the wall came tumbling down.

Everything happened just as God had said it would. With God's help Joshua led God's people to victory over the city of Jericho. They also kept their promise to Rahab. She and all her family were safe. Joshua was glad he had listened to God.

Gideon

Judges 6–7

God's people were known as the Israelites. They lived in the beautiful land of Canaan. Because it was such a nice place to live, other people wanted the land for themselves. Sometimes they tried to take the land from God's people. One of these groups, called the Midianites, did manage to take over the land. They made God's people slaves.

God wanted a leader for the Israelites who would help them. God picked a shy man named Gideon. God knew Gideon was the right person. When God's angel found Gideon, he was hiding grain from the Midianites.

God's angel talked to Gideon. The angel told him, "God is with you, mighty warrior. God has chosen you to be the leader of his people against the Midianites."

Gideon did not think he could do the things that God asked. "How can I save God's people?" Gideon wondered.

The angel said, "Go tear down the idols made for other gods." So Gideon tore down the idols.

Then Gideon asked, "Please give me a special sign so I will know God is with me. I will leave wool from a sheep on the ground. In the morning make the wool damp with dew but keep the ground dry. Then I will know that all these things that God asks are possible."

The next morning the ground was dry, and the wool was wet. Gideon wrung a whole bowl of water from the wool! God gave Gideon the sign, just as he had asked.

Even though God had given this sign, Gideon was still not sure. He said, "Please do not be angry. If I am the one to save your people, show me another sign. This time I will leave the wool out on the ground. When I get up in the morning, make the wool dry but the ground wet."

God made all these things happen just as Gideon had asked. So Gideon put a big army together. God told him, "The army is too big. I want to make sure that the people know I made this victory possible. First I want you to send home any men who are afraid." Gideon obeyed.

Then God said, "Send the remaining men to get a drink of water. You must separate those who lap water with their tongues like dogs from those who use their hands to drink." Gideon did as he was told. God chose the 300 men who lapped the water to fight the Midianites.

Then God told Gideon, "Now I will tell you the rest of the plan." So that night God told Gideon to gather the army. Everyone was to bring a torch, a jar, and a trumpet.

All the soldiers in Gideon's army covered their torches with a jar. Then they quietly climbed up the hillside and surrounded the Midianites' camp. It was very late and all the Midianites were asleep.

When Gideon gave the signal, the 300 men in his army blew their trumpets and smashed their jars on the ground. The Midianites had no idea what was going on! They were afraid. There was so much confusion inside the camp that the Midianites began to fight each other. Then they all ran away. Gideon's army chased the Midianites out of their country. God had kept his promise, and he let Gideon win the battle. The Israelites praised God.

Ruth and Naomi

Ruth 1–4

There once was a woman named Naomi. She and her husband had two sons. They all lived in Moab. But one day Naomi's husband died. She was very sad. "Now what should I do?" thought Naomi.

Then something else very sad happened. Naomi's son died. Her son was married to Ruth who lived in Moab, too. Now Ruth and Naomi were both alone. They were both unhappy. Naomi lived far from her family and she wanted to be with them.

So Naomi decided to return to the land where she grew up. She told Ruth, "You should return home and live with your mother and father. They will take care of you. And you will make a new life. God will watch over you."

Ruth was sad. She did not want to leave Naomi. Ruth loved Naomi very much. She said, "Please do not ask me to leave you. Where you go, I will go. Where you stay, I will stay. Your people will become my people and your God will be my God."

Naomi realized Ruth was determined to go with her. They hugged and Ruth said, "I could never leave you." Naomi was glad to have someone share her journey. They packed up all their belongings. Then Ruth and Naomi set out on the long trip to Bethlehem.

When Ruth and Naomi arrived in Bethlehem, it was harvest time. They were hungry, and they needed food. Ruth went to the fields to gather some grain. Because she was not from there, people noticed that she was different.

Boaz, the man who owned the fields, saw Ruth. He was curious about her, and he asked the workers who she was. "Her name is Ruth. She lives with Naomi," said the workers. They told him how hard she worked. Boaz knew Ruth was doing a good thing.

Then Boaz said to Ruth, "My workers have told me that you put Naomi's needs first and you are a hard worker.

You may gather grain from my field. I have told my workers to be nice to you. When you are thirsty, drink from my water jars." Ruth was grateful to Boaz. She thanked him for his kindness.

When all the workers in the field stopped to eat, Boaz made sure Ruth had food, too. In fact, he gave her so much food she had leftovers for Naomi. After they finished their meal, Ruth went back to the field to work. Boaz said to his workers, "I want you to leave extra grain for Ruth."

Boaz cared for Ruth. He thought she was very kind for taking care of Naomi. That night Ruth went home and showed Naomi all the grain she had gathered. Naomi was surprised and said, "Boaz is a good man to help us in our time of need. May God bless him."

Later Ruth and Boaz got married. They had a son and named him Obed. They asked Naomi to come live with them. And she did. God blessed all of them.

Hannah

1 Samuel 1 & 2

Hannah was married to a good man whose name was Elkanah. Even though he loved her, she was sad. More than anything in the world, she wanted to have a baby. But she could not. Some days she would cry and cry because she was so unhappy. Elkanah tried to comfort Hannah. Nothing he could do would make her feel better. When she saw other mothers with their children, she would become even more sad. Some days she would stop eating.

Elkanah asked Hannah, "Do you know I love you even if we do not have children?" But it did not matter. Hannah was still very sad.

Year after year, Hannah and Elkanah made a special trip to the temple so that they could worship God. They would pray and give thanks for all the blessings God had given to them. Other people went there to worship, too. One day at the temple, there was a mean woman. This woman had many children. She made fun of Hannah because she did not have any children. Hannah was more sad than ever.

Hannah was so unhappy on this day that she cried while she prayed. She was thinking how much she wanted to have a child. She asked God to give her a baby boy. Then Hannah made a promise to God. She promised if she could have a baby boy, the child would live at the temple and serve God as soon as he was old enough. Hannah repeated her promise to God in her heart again and again.

There was a priest named Eli at the door of the temple. Eli saw Hannah moving her lips, but he could not hear any sound coming out. He wondered, "What is going on?" He asked Hannah if she was feeling all right.

Hannah told Eli, "I am not sick. I am just very sad." She explained that she was praying to God with all her heart for something she wanted very much.

Eli listened to what Hannah said. He could tell this was really important to her. Eli wanted to make her feel better. He also knew what God wanted to do.

Eli said, "You may go home in peace, Hannah. May God hear your prayers and bless you with the son you are praying for." Hannah felt better. She went home. She began to eat again. Then she was not sad anymore.

In the morning Hannah and Elkanah went back to the temple. They praised God together, and then they returned to their home. God heard Hannah's prayers. The next year something very wonderful happened! Because of Hannah's faith, God answered her prayers and gave her a baby boy! Hannah was not sad anymore! She was glad God answered her prayers in this way. They even named the baby Samuel, which means, "I asked God for him."

Even though Hannah and Elkanah loved their son very much, Hannah did not forget her promise. She knew that when Samuel was old enough she would take him to stay with Eli. She wanted Samuel to learn everything there was to know about God's love and laws.

Samuel grew strong and healthy. He made Hannah very happy. Hannah knew it was time to keep her promise. When she packed Samuel's things, she also packed some gifts for God and Eli the priest. When the mother and son arrived at the temple, Hannah went to find Eli.

When Hannah found Eli, she told him who she was. Then she said, "I prayed for this child and God answered my prayer. Now I am here to do as I promised."

Hannah prayed again to tell God how happy she was. Again she thanked God for blessing her life with Samuel. Hannah kept her promise and dedicated Samuel's life from that day on to God's service.

Then God blessed Hannah even more. She had more children, three sons and two daughters. Hannah had kept her promise, and God blessed her.

Samuel

1 Samuel 1–3

When Samuel was a very young boy, he went to live at the temple with Eli. Samuel would study and talk with the teachers at the temple. There he learned the word of God.

One night something amazing happened! Samuel had already gone to sleep, but he was awakened when he heard a voice calling him. Samuel thought it was Eli. He ran into Eli's room. "Here I am," said Samuel.

Eli said to young Samuel, "I did not call you. Go back to bed and lie down."

Samuel went back to bed. Again he heard someone call his name. He ran back to Eli's room. "Here I am. You called me," said Samuel.

Once more Eli said, "No, I did not call you. Go back and lie down." Samuel was confused, but he obeyed Eli and went back to bed.

No sooner was Samuel back in his bed when the voice called out again. Samuel went to Eli once more. Then Eli realized it was the voice of God calling to Samuel. "My son," Eli said, "go and lie down. If the voice calls you again, say, 'Speak, God, for your servant is listening.'"

Samuel returned to bed. Soon he heard the voice calling him again. Samuel did as Eli told him. He said, "Speak, God, for your servant is listening."

God spoke to Samuel. The young boy listened carefully to everything that God had to say. In the morning Samuel opened the door to the temple. He was afraid to tell Eli what had happened.

Eli said to Samuel, "Do not be afraid. Tell me what God said to you." Eli knew it was important to hear the message God had given Samuel. So Samuel told Eli everything God had said.

God often spoke to Samuel after that night. He had a very important job. Samuel served as a prophet of God. After God would speak to him, he would talk to God's people. He would tell them what God said.

David and Goliath

1 Samuel 16–17

God told the prophet Samuel to travel to the town of Bethlehem. God said to him, "You will find a man named Jesse. I have chosen one of his sons to be the new king."

Samuel did as God asked. When he got to Bethlehem, he asked Jesse to bring his sons to him. Samuel shook his head. "No," he said. "The one God has chosen is not here. Do you have any more sons?"

"Yes," replied Jesse. "David, the youngest, is still tending the sheep." Jesse sent for David.

As David approached, God said, "He is the one." Samuel told Jesse that one day David would be the new king.

David was a very good boy. He liked to run, jump, and play like other little boys. David also loved to play his harp and sing songs while he cared for his sheep.

One day Saul, the king of Israel, did not feel very well. He sent one of his helpers to Jesse. The helper said, "Jesse, the king wants your son David to play his harp and sing for him. The king will not eat and he will not talk with anyone. He thinks that David's music will make him feel better." Jesse was pleased with the king's request.

So Jesse sent David and a donkey loaded with wonderful gifts to give to King Saul. The king liked David very much. Soon David's beautiful music filled the whole palace. The music made the king feel better right away. The king said, "David, there is no one in the kingdom who can play the harp like you."

One day an enemy army came to take over King Saul's land. The king called for the people to make an army. They would protect the land. Three of David's brothers joined King Saul's army. But the king did not ask David. The king thought David was too young and too small to be a soldier. "I must send you home, David," the king said. "You helped me so much by playing music, but I do not want you here during the fighting. My helper will take you home."

David was not happy at all. He wanted to be with his brothers and fight the enemy. When he got home he told his father, "I can fight. Remember when I saved the sheep from the lion?"

"Yes," David's father said patiently. "I do remember, but I need you here at home to help tend the sheep." He knew his father was right, but David was still unhappy.

Jesse knew young David had a good heart. He called to David and said, "Your brothers have been away for awhile. They will need more food." David's heart jumped. He was excited about going to see his brothers. He missed them, and he wondered what was happening at the battle.

Very early the next morning, Jesse loaded up a donkey with food. David set out on his journey. As he got closer to the valley, he could see where King Saul's army had set up camp. As he came closer, David could see the two armies as they faced off against each other. King Saul's army was on one side and the enemy's army was on the other. David finally arrived at Saul's camp. He ran to his brothers and said, "Father sent me to bring you this food."

Just as David greeted his brothers, some of the soldiers shouted out loud, "There he is. There is Goliath!" Puzzled, David looked to see what they were talking about. On the other side stood the biggest man he had ever seen! He was coming out of the enemy camp. The giant was almost 10 feet tall. He was covered with armor from head to toe. The giant looked toward King Saul's tent.

Then the giant roared, "I am Goliath. I will fight any of you. If you beat me, our army will be your slaves. But if I beat you, you will be our slaves forever!"

King Saul's soldiers looked at Goliath. They shook with fear. But the giant did not scare David. The soldiers even heard little David say, "I am not afraid. I will fight the giant." The soldiers told the king what he said.

The king heard someone wanted to fight the giant. The soldiers brought David in front of the king. King Saul asked, "David, are you the one who wants to fight Goliath?"

David said, "Yes, King Saul."

The king said, "David, you are just a young shepherd boy. You are not trained for battle."

David said, "The job of a shepherd is to protect his sheep. I have saved my sheep from a lion. With God's help, I can save us from the giant." No one else wanted to fight the giant. So the king agreed to let David fight Goliath. King Saul wanted to protect David, so he gave the boy his armor to keep him safe.

After trying it on, David said, "Your armor is too heavy for me. I must fight him my own way. God will help and protect me."

Then David ran over to a nearby stream. He chose several smooth stones to use with his sling. David placed one of the stones inside the sling. Then he ran back. "I am here to fight you, Goliath," David shouted.

When the giant saw David he laughed. "Little boy, you are like a little grasshopper to me!" Goliath continued his roar, "Do you really expect to fight me? Do you think I am a dog and you can beat me with your sticks and stones?"

David looked closely at the giant. He was covered with heavy armor. David found a spot on his forehead where he would take aim. "I am not afraid of you, Goliath. You come with your shield and sword, but I come with the strength of God," shouted David.

David's words made Goliath angry. He reached for his sword. King Saul's army was silent. They watched David as he ran toward the giant. He swung his sling over his head. Round and round it went. Then he let the stone fly. It flew straight into Goliath's forehead. And Goliath fell down.

King Saul's army cheered out loud! "We have won the battle!" they shouted. "David has defeated Goliath!" When the enemy saw that Goliath had been defeated, they began running away! King Saul's army chased after them.

After the battle was over, the king called David in front of the soldiers. "David," said Saul, "you were not afraid. You trusted God, and he gave you the strength to defeat the giant Goliath." Everyone cheered for David.

David thanked God for giving him the courage to fight the giant and win.

Solomon

1 Kings 1–8

David had many sons. Several of his sons tried to become king. But David discovered their plans and stopped them. Then he chose his youngest son, Solomon, to be the new king. David called for a big celebration. There was a grand parade with trumpets and lots of soldiers.

David had Solomon ride on a special mule throughout the city. As Solomon did this, everyone cheered! They celebrated their new king. "Long live Solomon," the people shouted. "Long live the king."

When King David was very old, he called Solomon to his bedside. He said, "Soon it will be time for me to leave this earth. I am counting on you to be a strong leader. You must promise to obey God's laws. You must also keep each one of his commandments."

David continued his instructions to Solomon, "If you do this, God will watch over you. He will take care of you and give you everything you need. But this will happen only if you and your children follow God's ways."

Solomon followed David's advice, and God was very pleased with him. God was so happy with Solomon that one night as Solomon was sleeping, he came to him in a dream. "Solomon," God said, "what can I give you?"

Solomon replied, "God, you have made me king over your people. In fact, I rule over so many people, I cannot even count all of them. Please give me wisdom to know right from wrong so that I can help them."

God answered, "Solomon, your request pleases me very much. You could have asked for wealth, power, or long life, but you did not. You asked for wisdom to know right from wrong, and I will give this to you. But I will also give you riches and honor. You will be the most powerful king on the earth as long as you live." Solomon awoke and realized he had been dreaming.

Solomon never forgot what his father, King David, had told him. He always asked God for help. And he followed God's rules. Solomon ruled God's people with such great wisdom that people from all over came to hear him speak.

Sometimes Solomon would recite wise sayings or even sing songs. He would teach about birds, plants, and animals. No man had ever had such great wisdom. There was always plenty of food to eat. The people in Solomon's kingdom lived in peace. God blessed Solomon many times over, and his kingdom kept growing and growing.

"I want God to know that we are thankful for all that he does for us," said Solomon. "I am going to build a great temple for God where my people can worship him."

For seven years the best craftsmen in King Solomon's kingdom worked to build the temple. There was a special room in the temple for God's commandments. This room was the most important room. The king also had all of the inside walls, floors, and altars of the temple covered with gold. He did all these things to honor and thank God for all the blessings he had been given.

When the hard work was finished and the temple was ready, King Solomon gathered all his people together. They watched as the Ark of the Covenant, which contained God's commandments, was placed in the temple. Solomon raised his hands and blessed the people. He reminded them of all the wonderful things God provided for them. There was a great celebration. Everyone at the temple joined together to praise and worship God.

Elijah

1 Kings 1–17

Wise King Solomon ruled God's people for many years. He followed God's laws, and God blessed Solomon in many ways. Solomon even built a temple for God so the people in his kingdom would have a place to worship God.

After Solomon was no longer king, other kings came into power. Many of these kings did not believe in God. They did not follow the laws. Instead of worshiping God, they worshiped statues made of wood and stone. Then they told the people to do the same. This made God sad.

One of the kings who did not worship God was named Ahab. King Ahab did not follow God's laws. He worshiped statues instead of God. Ahab was always doing wrong things. This made God sad and angry.

So God chose a prophet named Elijah to do an important job. God told Elijah to go talk to King Ahab. Elijah had to remind King Ahab about the difference between right and wrong.

So Elijah went to see King Ahab as God asked. Elijah said, "Because you have forgotten what is right, the one true God has decided there will be no rain or dew for a very long time." Elijah knew God wanted Ahab to see his power. God wanted Ahab to follow his laws.

After he finished giving the message to the king, Elijah was kept safe by God. Since God would not let it rain for a long time, there would be very little water. Without water, the plants could not grow. And without rain, it would even be hard to find water to drink.

But God took care of his prophet Elijah and said, "You must leave this land. I will show you a place where there is a brook. The land will not have rain, but you will have water to drink from the brook."

God showed Elijah this secret place. He said, "Do not worry. I will send birds called ravens. They will bring you food to eat." Elijah did exactly as God told him. He found the brook just as God said. And each morning and evening the ravens brought him food to eat.

It had not rained for a very long time. Even the brook Elijah drank from began to dry up. Now there was no water left for him to drink. But Elijah did not worry. He knew everything would be okay. God continued to keep watch over Elijah. God told him, "You will go to a small town. When you get there, you will find a woman at the city gate. The woman will give you food to eat."

Again Elijah did as he was told and traveled to the town. At the gate of the town there was the woman. Elijah asked her for a drink of water. He also asked for some bread to eat. The woman said, "I do not have any bread. I only have a little flour and oil."

Elijah believed God's words. He knew God would take care of them. Elijah said, "Do not be afraid. If you do what I ask, there will be plenty of food." He told the woman at the gate exactly what to do.

"First bake me a small loaf of bread," he instructed her. "There will be enough for you to make bread for yourself and your son. God will take care of us and make sure there is enough flour and oil until it rains again."

The woman believed all the things Elijah told her. She baked the bread. And just as Elijah had said, there was enough flour and oil to make food for all three of them.

Elijah stayed with the woman and her son. Each day God gave them food to eat. One day the woman's son got sick. He was very ill. Suddenly the boy stopped breathing. The woman was very sad and upset. She said, "Elijah, why did this happen to my son?"

Elijah wanted to help. He took her son upstairs. There he prayed to God. He asked God to give the boy life again. And God heard Elijah's prayers.

Elijah brought the boy back to his mother. The woman was very happy to have her son back! The mother and son hugged each other. Then she said, "Now I know that you speak the truth. I believe your God is the true God."

Josiah

2 Kings 22 & 23

Many kings did not obey God. Some worshiped gold or wooden idols. There were some kings who worshiped the sun, and others even worshiped the stars. Over time they tried to destroy all the written copies of the Book of Law. The Book of Law contained all the rules that God gave his people. When the kings stopped obeying God, the people stopped, too. These things made God sad.

Then one day a new king came into power. This king was different from the other kings. His name was Josiah, and he was only eight years old.

As Josiah grew older, he became a good ruler for his people. He always tried to do what was best for them.

When Josiah was 26 years old, he made repairs to the temple where people went to pray. "We will take all of the money collected at the door of the temple and use it to buy wood and stone," he told his helpers. "We will hire honest workers to make the temple beautiful again." Josiah's helpers were so honest, he did not even have to watch to see how they spent the temple's money.

One day a priest working at the temple discovered an old scroll. He took it to King Josiah and read aloud from the scroll. It was a copy of the Book of Law. It contained all the rules that God had given his people.

When Josiah heard the rules from the Book of Law, he became very upset. He said, "We have not followed God's law. We must try to find out what we can do to make things right with God."

King Josiah's officers took the Book of Law to a wise woman. They hoped she could help them figure out what to do. When the woman finished reading the Book of Law, she told them, "God is unhappy with the kings who ruled over the land before Josiah. But God is pleased that Josiah is trying so hard to do what is right. God will not punish Josiah or his people as long as he rules."

Josiah wanted all his people to know about God's law. He asked them to come to the temple. When they were all inside, he read them the entire Book of Law. The people were afraid. They promised to follow the law.

Josiah made the promise, too. He tried his best to keep his word. Whenever he saw something in his kingdom that God did not like, he changed it. Josiah had all the old idols burned. The people in his kingdom stopped worshiping the stars and sun. God was happy that young Josiah kept his promise. So God watched over Josiah and took care of him and his people.

Esther

Esther 1–10

There once was a rich and powerful king whose name was Xerxes. King Xerxes had many wonderful things. But he did not have a queen. Many beautiful women came to meet the king. Each one dreamed she might be the new queen. They went through months of preparation before they were introduced to the king.

One day the king met a beautiful young woman named Esther. He thought she was the most beautiful woman in all the land. The king knew that Esther would become his queen. But there was much to be done before she could be crowned. It took nearly a year to get everything ready.

During the year Esther stayed at the palace. Until then she had lived with her cousin Mordecai. He had raised her and loved her very much. Mordecai trusted and believed in God. He taught Esther to love God, too.

Finally the big day came, and the king carefully placed the crown on Esther's head. She was now Queen Esther. Mordecai was very happy. Every day he came to the palace gate to talk to Esther. He wanted to be sure that she was happy and safe.

One day, while Mordecai waited at the gate for Esther, he heard two of the king's guards talking. They did not like the king and wanted to get rid of him. Mordecai knew he must stop them. He did not want the king to be hurt. He had to get a secret message to Queen Esther.

Mordecai waited for Queen Esther to come to the gate. He knew he had to tell her about the guards' plan to hurt the king. As Esther approached, Mordecai whispered, "You must help save the king. Two of his guards are planning to get rid of him. They do not want him to be king anymore."

Esther told the king about the plan to hurt him. Then she said, "Mordecai warned me of this danger. He wants to make sure you are not harmed."

The king sent out some of his officers. They discovered that what Queen Esther said was true. The king was happy that Mordecai had saved him. The king had a palace servant write these things in a record book just as they happened. Now everyone would know how Mordecai saved the king.

Later a mean person named Haman was given a very important job by the king. He became one of the king's highest officers. To honor Haman, the king made a law for the people in the kingdom to follow. According to the law, whenever Haman passed by, everyone had to bow down to him. Haman was very pleased with the new law. It made him feel important when people bowed down to him.

But there was one man who refused to bow to Haman. That man was Mordecai, Esther's cousin. Haman was very angry when Mordecai would not bow to him. He wanted to get rid of Mordecai and all his people. Haman knew the king would never let him harm Mordecai for not bowing to him. So Haman came up with a plan.

Haman went to the king. He said, "King Xerxes, some of the people in your kingdom are bad. They do not obey your laws. You must get rid of them. I will give you money to pay for this." The king agreed with Haman. He sent out his men to tell the people of the new law.

Mordecai cried when he heard Haman's horrible plan. The new law meant Haman could get rid of Mordecai and all his people. All of Mordecai's people were afraid.

When Queen Esther learned about Haman's plan from Mordecai, she was afraid, too. Mordecai wanted her to see the king, but the law said no one could see the king unless they were called for or they might lose their life. Esther knew that she had to try to save her people. So she came up with a plan.

Esther stood in the palace hall so that the king would be sure to see her. The king did see Esther. He was happy. He motioned for her to come to him. The king said, "If you ask for half my kingdom, I will gladly give it to you."

Esther quickly replied, "I would like you and Haman to dine with me today." The king was very pleased at this and granted Esther's wish.

When Haman ate dinner with the king and queen that night, he was very happy. Haman did not know Queen Esther was Mordecai's cousin. At the end of the meal, the king asked Esther if she had any requests of him. She said, "I would like to prepare another meal for you and Haman tomorrow." Again the king granted her wish.

That night the king could not sleep. A servant brought his record book. "Read to me," said the king. He read the part about when Mordecai saved the king's life. "How did I thank Mordecai for this?" the king asked.

The servant said, "Nothing was done."

The next day Haman returned to the palace. The king asked him, "How would you honor a person who made the king happy?"

Haman thought Xerxes was talking about him. Haman said, "I would give the person a beautiful robe, put him on a horse, and lead him through the kingdom while someone calls out, 'This person has done great things for the king.'"

"Then go find Mordecai, and do all these things for him at once!" the king ordered Haman. Haman was not happy, but he had to obey the king.

By the end of the day, Haman was very angry. But he returned to the palace for his dinner with Esther and King Xerxes. As they finished their meal the king said, "Esther, if you ask for half of my kingdom, I will gladly give it to you."

Queen Esther said to the king, "If you love me, do not harm me or my people."

The king asked, "Who would do such a thing?" When Esther told the king of Haman's plan, he was so angry that he left the room. Haman asked Esther to help him, but this just made the king more angry. He had Haman taken away. Then the king wrote a new law to protect Esther's people.

Queen Esther called Mordecai before her. She said to him, "Our people are safe." The king gave Haman's job to Mordecai. Everyone celebrated! Esther was very brave. She was glad she had risked her life to save her people.

Shadrach, Meshach, and Abednego

Daniel 3

The King of Babylon decided to build the biggest idol in all the land. When it was completed, the large idol stood 90 feet tall and 9 feet wide. It was made of gold. The king wanted everyone in his kingdom to worship his shiny new idol.

So the king made a new law. Then he called all the people in his kingdom together and announced his new law. He instructed them, "Whenever you hear the sound of the horn, the flute, and the harp, you must bow down and worship the golden idol. Anyone who does not bow down will be thrown into a fiery furnace."

170

As soon as the music began to play, the people bowed down to the golden idol. Everyone bowed down except three men who worked for the king. They were Shadrach, Meshach, and Abednego. They believed in the true God, and they would not worship the idol. Some people in the kingdom noticed Shadrach, Meshach, and Abednego would not bow down to the idol. They went to the king and said, "We follow your rules, and we bow to your statue of gold. But there are three men who refuse to bow down. They are disobeying your laws."

"Who are these men?" asked the king. The people told him they were Shadrach, Meshach, and Abednego.

The king was very angry. "Bring them to me," said the king. "Let me talk to these men."

Shadrach, Meshach, and Abednego came and stood in front of the king. The king knew they worshiped God, not idols. He told them his new law one more time. Then he said, "If you do not bow down when the music plays, you will be tossed into the fiery furnace."

The three men said, "There is no need for you to play your music. We will not bow down to your idol. We will only worship the one true God. Our God will save us from the flames. Even if we are not saved, it is important for you to know that this is what we believe. We will not worship your idol."

The king was really mad at them! He told the soldiers, "Heat the furnace seven times hotter than usual." Then he told his strongest soldiers to tie up Shadrach, Meshach, and Abednego and throw them into the hot fire.

The soldiers tied Shadrach, Meshach, and Abednego's hands and took them to the furnace. It was very, very hot. Then the guards threw them into the fire.

Suddenly the king jumped right out of his seat. "Wait a minute!" he exclaimed. "We only threw three men into the furnace. Now I see four people walking around in the fire! The fourth one looks like an angel. And look! Their hands are no longer tied, and they do not seem to be harmed."

The guards looked into the scorching flames. The king was right! An angel of God had come into the furnace and made sure Shadrach, Meshach, and Abednego stayed safe. The king shouted into the blaze, "Shadrach, Meshach, and Abednego, come out of there right now!"

Shadrach, Meshach, and Abednego came out of the hot, fiery furnace. Everyone gathered around them to see what had happened. They were very surprised to see that not a hair on their heads or a thread of their clothing had been touched by the flames of the fire. They did not even smell like smoke! No one could believe what they saw.

"Let us give praise to the God of Shadrach, Meshach, and Abednego," said the king. "They had such strong faith that they would rather face a fiery furnace than bow down to a golden idol. Their God must be the one true God."

The king made a new law right then. "No one should say anything bad about the God of Shadrach, Meshach, and Abednego. If they do, they shall be punished," declared the king. "There is no other god who can save his people like the God of Shadrach, Meshach, and Abednego."

Daniel

Daniel 6

A new king came to power in Babylon. His name was King Darius. Darius had a very large kingdom. One day he appointed three wise rulers to help take care of his people. One of these rulers was Daniel.

Daniel was a very hard worker. He always did a good job, and the people trusted him. King Darius liked Daniel. The king also noticed that Daniel prayed to his God three times each day. One day King Darius decided to put Daniel in charge of his kingdom. Once Daniel was in charge, only the king would be more powerful than he.

When some of the other rulers who worked for King Darius heard about the king's decision, they were jealous. Many other people who worked for King Darius were jealous, too. They did not want the king to be proud of Daniel. They wanted the king to be proud of them. They tried to think of some way to make the king angry at Daniel.

"We will never make Daniel look bad," said the first ruler. "He always does a good job."

They thought and thought. Then the second ruler said, "Maybe we can get him into trouble because he is always praying to his God."

"I think you are right," said one of the king's workers. They came up with a plan. Then they went to see the king.

"King Darius, may you live forever," said the rulers as they stood before him. "We have written a new law, and we want you to sign it. This law says for the next 30 days no person in your kingdom can pray to any other man or God. They can only ask things of you. Anyone who does not obey this law must be thrown into the lions' den."

King Darius liked the new law. He liked the idea that only he could grant his people their requests. King Darius signed the law. Then he decided to announce the signing of his new law to his people. He sent out his helpers to tell everyone in his kingdom the news. The rulers were happy that their plan was working. They ran to Daniel's house to see what he would do about the new law.

When Daniel first heard about the law he did not know what to do. "Maybe I should stop praying. After all, the law is only for 30 days," he thought. But Daniel knew it would be wrong to stop praying to God. "If I put my trust in God," thought Daniel, "I am sure he will take care of me."

That evening Daniel knelt down and said his prayers as usual. When the other rulers saw him pray, they ran to tell the king. "King Darius!" they cried. "Someone broke your law!" The king wanted to know who it was. "It is Daniel," they shouted. "You must throw him to the lions."

The king knew he had been tricked. He tried and tried to think of a way to save Daniel, but he could not. He called for Daniel and said, "You have broken the law, and I cannot help you." The guards threw Daniel in the lions' den. Daniel prayed to God. He asked God to take care of him.

The king could not sleep that night because he was so worried about Daniel. As soon as the sun came up, King Darius ran to see if his friend was still alive. When the king got to the lions' den he shouted, "Daniel, has your God saved you? Are you safe, my friend?"

"Yes, King!" Daniel shouted back. "I am alive! God sent an angel to close the mouths of the lions. I am safe."

King Darius was happy! He ordered that Daniel be removed from the den. They were glad to see each other. Daniel was safe because he trusted God.

Right away King Darius issued a new law. The law told everyone about God. It also told how God saved Daniel by protecting him from the lions. The king wanted everyone to know the wonderful things God did to protect Daniel.

Jonah

Jonah 1–4

Jonah was a prophet. A prophet is someone who gives messages to people from God. God said to Jonah, "I want you to go to the city of Nineveh. You will tell the people there to stop doing bad things."

Jonah did not want to go to Nineveh. The people there were bad, and Jonah did not like them. He did not know why God wanted to help them. Even Jonah's friends knew that the people from Nineveh were bad. They did not like them either. So Jonah decided to run away. He got on a ship that would take him far, far away from Nineveh.

Jonah could not hide from God. Shortly after the ship set sail, God sent a great storm. Jonah did not know about the storm because he was asleep below deck. The wind from the storm was so strong that it shook the whole ship back and forth in the water.

The captain and the sailors were afraid the ship would break apart. The sailors began tossing things overboard to lighten the load, but that did not help. One of the sailors asked, "What is causing this storm?"

No one knew. They tried calling upon their gods to stop the storm, but the storm just grew bigger. One of the sailors remembered that Jonah was on board. He had told the sailors that he was running away from God. The ship's captain went to Jonah and said, "How can you sleep? You must call on your God. Maybe he will protect us."

The sea was getting rougher and rougher. The sailors were very frightened. They asked, "What can we do to make the storm go away?"

Jonah knew that God was unhappy with him. He said, "God sent the storm because I ran away from him. If you throw me overboard, the storm will stop."

The sailors did not want to throw Jonah into the water. They tried to row the ship back to shore, but they could not. The storm grew even stronger. Finally the sailors knew what they must do. First they prayed to Jonah's God that they would not be harmed. Then they threw Jonah into the sea. The sailors were still afraid.

Suddenly the storm stopped. The sea grew calm. God saved Jonah by sending a big fish to swallow him.

Jonah was inside the big fish for three days and three nights. While Jonah was inside the fish, he had lots of time to think and lots of time to pray.

"Please help me God. I am sorry for trying to run away from you," Jonah prayed. "Please give me another chance. You have been good to me. I will do anything you tell me."

God heard Jonah's prayers. God told the fish to spit Jonah out onto dry land. The big fish followed God's

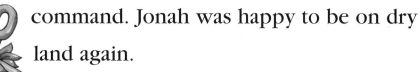

command. Jonah was happy to be on dry land again.

"You must go to Nineveh," God said to Jonah a second time. This time Jonah obeyed God. He went to Nineveh.

God had given Jonah a big job. Nineveh was a very big city. It was so big that it took three days for Jonah to walk through the whole city. As he walked, he would tell people God's message. Jonah said, "People of Nineveh, stop doing bad things."

The people listened to what Jonah said. They believed his words. They were sorry for all the bad things they had done. They wanted to do what was right.

Even the king was sorry. He called all the people in his kingdom together. He told the people to pray to God for forgiveness. The whole city of Nineveh prayed as the king said. God was pleased that the people of Nineveh listened to the message he had given Jonah. The king and his people were happy, too.

Stories from
the New Testament

Mary and Joseph

Luke 1–2

God had a special plan. The plan began with God sending his angel Gabriel to deliver a message to a young woman named Mary. She was soon to be married to a carpenter. The carpenter's name was Joseph.

When Mary saw Gabriel, she was afraid. Gabriel said, "Do not be afraid. You have been chosen to have God's Son. You will name him Jesus." Mary was confused. She was wondering how this could happen. "You must trust God. All things are possible with him," said Gabriel.

"I do love God. I will trust him, and I will do whatever he says," Mary said. Then the angel left.

There was a ruler who wanted to count all of his people. So everyone was told to return to the town where their family was born. Joseph's family was from the town called Bethlehem, so he and Mary had to travel there. Mary and Joseph prepared for their long journey.

When they arrived in Bethlehem, every house was full. Mary was going to have the baby soon, so they looked for a safe place to stay. Mary and Joseph looked everywhere, but all the inns were full. Finally one innkeeper said, "You can stay in my stable with the animals. It is all I can offer you, but at least you will have a safe place to sleep."

That night Mary and Joseph stayed in the stable. Then something wonderful happened. Just as the angel Gabriel had promised, Mary gave birth to a baby boy. They named the baby Jesus.

Mary and Joseph lovingly wrapped the baby Jesus in soft clothes. Then they filled a manger with fresh hay to make a bed for Jesus. Mary placed the baby Jesus into the manger. He slept peacefully as Mary and Joseph watched over him.

God placed a bright, beautiful star in the sky. The star was seen shining high above the city of Bethlehem. The tail of the star pointed to the place where the newborn baby lay quietly sleeping.

Outside the city in a nearby field, shepherds watched over their sheep. Suddenly a bright light appeared. They were very afraid. This had never happened to them before. They covered their eyes to protect them from the bright light. The shepherds were so frightened, they could not talk.

It was an angel. The angel said, "Do not be afraid. I am bringing you good news. This is wonderful news for all the people. Today in Bethlehem God's Son has been born. When you find the baby Jesus, he will be wrapped in soft clothes and lying in a manger."

Then the night sky was filled with angels from heaven. They praised God and said, "Glory to God in the highest, and peace on earth." Then the angels went back to heaven.

The shepherds were very excited. They were happy to hear that God's Son had been born. They said, "Let us go visit this baby that the angels told us about. We must go to Bethlehem and see all these wonderful things ourselves."

So the shepherds left their sheep and hurried to the city of Bethlehem. They found the stable and went inside. There the shepherds found the baby lying in a manger just as the angel had said. They bowed before the baby and worshiped him. They thanked God for sending baby Jesus.

The shepherds returned to their flocks. They praised God for all the things they had seen and heard. They told everyone about this special night.

Jesus at the Temple

Matthew 2 & Luke 2

One day after Jesus was born, Mary and Joseph took the baby to the temple. There was a very old man named Simeon in the temple that day. He knew he would live to see God's Son. When Simeon saw Jesus, he took the baby into his arms and said, "All of my life I have waited for you to come."

Simeon praised baby Jesus, then he sang a sweet song to him. Simeon told Mary and Joseph that Jesus was the savior of the world.

Later three wise men traveled to Jerusalem. They were looking for the newborn king. They knew he was God's Son. They followed a bright star, and it led them to the city of Bethlehem. When the three wise men saw baby Jesus, he was with his mother, Mary. They said, "A bright star has guided us to your house. We have traveled for two years to see God's Son."

Then the wise men bowed down and worshiped baby Jesus. They gave him gifts of gold, sweet smelling perfume, and the finest herbs. Then the wise men left baby Jesus. They returned to their homes. And like the shepherds, they told everyone they met about God's Son.

Jesus grew up in the town of Nazareth. He grew to be strong and wise. Every year Mary, Joseph, and Jesus took a long trip. They would go to the temple in Jerusalem for a festival. They traveled with all their family and friends.

When Jesus was 12 years old, his family once again made the trip to Jerusalem. After the festival, they started the trip home. But Jesus stayed behind. When Mary and Joseph realized that Jesus was not with them, they began searching for him. For three days they looked for him. But they could not find Jesus anywhere. They went back to the temple to ask the teachers if they had seen him.

When Mary and Joseph got to the temple, they found Jesus. He was sitting in the temple and talking with the teachers. The teachers were truly amazed at this little boy. He understood new and wonderful things about God. The teachers liked him because he asked them questions and talked to them about God's laws.

Mary said, "Jesus, we have been looking everywhere for you. We were worried about you."

"Why were you looking for me, mother? Did you not know I would be at my Father's house?" replied Jesus.

Mary did not understand, but she was glad that Jesus was safe. Then Mary, Joseph, and Jesus returned to their home in Nazareth.

Mary and Joseph did not always understand why Jesus did things. But they loved him very much. They knew he was God's Son and that God had very special plans for Jesus. They had fun watching him as he grew taller and stronger. They saw his love for God grow stronger, too.

Jesus obeyed his parents, and he was a good child. He listened to his mother's words. Joseph taught Jesus about being a carpenter. Jesus became a good helper. He loved Mary and Joseph. They shared many happy days together.

John the Baptist

Luke 1 & 3, Matthew 3

Elizabeth and Zachariah had been married for a long time. They were very old. They often prayed that God would give them a child. They knew they could not have a baby, and this made them very sad.

Elizabeth and Zachariah loved and worshiped God, and God was very pleased with them. Zachariah was a priest who worked in the temple. His job was to enter a special room and light the sweet smelling herbs for worship called incense. One day as Zachariah was lighting the incense, an angel appeared to him.

Zachariah was frightened by the angel. "Do not be afraid," the angel said. "I bring good news for you. Your prayers have been heard. You and your wife, Elizabeth, will have a son. You are to name him John. When John grows up, he will talk to many people and teach them to love God. This will prepare the people for the arrival of God's Son, Jesus." The angel's words made Zachariah very happy. But he could not believe what he heard. He wondered how he would know if this was true.

The angel said, "God sent me to tell you this news. But since you do not believe me, you will not be able to speak until the day your baby is born." Then the angel was gone.

Outside the temple, people were gathering to pray. Zachariah came out and tried to tell them what happened. But just as the angel had said, he could not speak.

While Zachariah and Elizabeth waited for the birth of their baby John, Mary was waiting for Jesus to be born. One day she visited her cousin Elizabeth. "Hello," she called to Elizabeth as she arrived. At that moment the baby in Elizabeth's tummy jumped. Elizabeth knew that Mary had been touched by God in a special way.

"God has blessed you and your child," Elizabeth said.

The day came when Zachariah and Elizabeth's baby was born. Friends and family had gathered to celebrate. Everyone was talking and laughing except Zachariah. He still could not speak. People began to say that the baby should be named after Zachariah. Zachariah shook his head no and motioned for a writing tablet. Then he wrote, "His name is John." Suddenly Zachariah's mouth opened. He said, "His name is John." He could talk again!

John grew up and loved God very much. He spent all of his days serving God. He lived in the desert. For clothes he wore camel's hair. He also wore a leather belt. Most of the time he ate locusts and wild honey for food.

God was with John. John spent his days telling others that God was about to send someone special to them. That person was God's Son, Jesus.

Many people listened to John. They tried to obey God's rules. John took these people to the Jordan River and baptized them. He did this by dipping them in the water. This baptism showed their friends and neighbors that they loved God. As John did this he said, "I baptize you with water. Someone else is coming. He will baptize you with God's Spirit."

John was talking about Jesus. He wanted people to know Jesus was coming.

One day Jesus came to the Jordan River. "John, I want you to baptize me," said Jesus.

John was surprised and said, "You are God's Son. I am not good enough to tie your sandals, yet you ask me to baptize you. It would be better if you baptized me!"

But Jesus said, "I must do what is right." So John baptized Jesus.

After Jesus was baptized, God's spirit appeared in the form of a dove. It came down from heaven and landed on Jesus. Then God's voice from heaven was heard. He said, "You are my Son. I love you. I am pleased with you."

Calling the Disciples

Luke 5 & 6

Jesus knew God loved him and was very pleased with him. So he went to the desert. Jesus knew God had a plan for him and would take care of him. He stayed there for 40 days and did not even take any food. Jesus asked God for special friends. Jesus wanted to teach them about God.

After Jesus left the desert, he spent much of his time telling people about God's love. In one town, Jesus healed many sick people. The news of how Jesus healed people spread. More and more people came to see Jesus.

One day Jesus went to the Sea of Galilee. The crowd that came to see Jesus grew larger and larger. Jesus saw two boats on the beach. They were left there by fishermen who were washing their nets. Jesus stepped into the boat belonging to a fisherman named Peter. Then he asked Peter to push the boat out into the water, just a short distance from the shore. Peter did as he was asked. Now it would be easier for the people to hear what Jesus had to say.

After Jesus finished speaking, he said to Peter, "Go out farther in the sea and throw your nets into the water. You will catch fish."

Peter answered, "We have been fishing all day, and we have not caught anything." But he did as Jesus said.

When Peter and Andrew pulled their nets up from the water, they were very surprised. Even though they had not caught a single fish all day, their nets were now full. They called two other fishermen, James and his brother John, to bring another boat so they could bring in all the fish. Now both of the boats were so full of fish they began to sink!

Peter knew Jesus had filled his nets with fish. When they landed the boat on the shore, Peter fell to his knees and said, "Please go away. I have done many bad things. I am not good enough."

"Do not be afraid. From now on you will be a fisher of men," said Jesus. Andrew also stopped fishing and began to follow Jesus. Then Jesus called to the other fishermen, James and John, to join him. They too left their nets and followed Jesus.

Later Jesus walked by a tax office. The tax offices were used to collect money from the people. The tax collectors gave the money to the king. Sometimes the tax collectors took more money than was owed. They would keep the extra money for themselves.

The man who worked in this tax collection office was named Matthew. Jesus looked at Matthew and said, "Follow me." Matthew dropped the money he was holding, and he walked away from his tax office to follow Jesus.

Jesus knew that there was a lot of work for him to do on earth. He chose 12 men to help him spread the word of God. The 12 men he chose were Peter, Andrew, James, John, Philip, Bartholomew, Matthew, Thomas, Thaddaeus, Simon, another helper named James, and Judas.

Jesus called these 12 men his disciples. They would travel with him and listen as he taught about God's love. Jesus wanted them to listen and learn about God so that one day they would also teach people about God's love.

The Wedding Miracle

John 2

Now Jesus had 12 men to travel with him. They went to many cities. The disciples listened to Jesus as he taught the people how God wanted them to live. He would tell them things about God that he did not tell anyone else.

One day Jesus and his disciples were visiting the city of Cana. They were invited to a wedding party. Mary, Jesus' mother, was also at the party. At that celebration Jesus did something that he had never done before. He performed his first miracle.

People came from all over to attend the wedding. The party would last for many days. The bride and groom and their families served food and wine to all their guests. They would serve their best food and wine during the first few days of the party. It took a lot of food and drink to feed so many people for all those days.

During the party Jesus' mother noticed that there was no more wine. "Jesus," Mary said, "the wine is gone, and the party is not over."

"Mother, it is not time yet," said Jesus.

Mary told the servants, "Listen to Jesus, and do as he asks. He will tell you what needs to be done."

Jesus walked over to six huge water jars. Each jar held nearly 30 gallons of water. Jesus turned to the servants and said, "Fill these jars to the top with water." The servants did as they were told.

Then Jesus said, "Now fill a cup from this jar and give it to the servant who is in charge and ask him to drink the wine." The servers did not understand why they were to do this, but they did as Jesus asked. They dipped a cup in the water until it was full. Then they took it to the servant in charge. He drank it.

When the servant in charge took a drink from the cup, he was very surprised! "This is the best wine I have ever tasted," he exclaimed. The servants who had filled the jars with water were amazed. Jesus had turned the water into wine! All six jars were now full of wine.

The servant went to the groom. "Sir," he said, "at most weddings the best food and drink is served during the first few days of the wedding party, but you have saved the best wine for last!" The other servants knew Jesus had turned the water into wine. The 12 disciples had seen the miracle, too. They were amazed that Jesus had done this. It was his first miracle.

Planting Seeds

Matthew 13

Everyone wanted to see Jesus. They loved listening to the stories he told. One day Jesus was sitting by the Sea of Galilee. There were people everywhere who had come to hear him speak. Jesus wanted to make sure they could hear him. So he got into a boat and pushed it a little way out on the water. Then Jesus told this story.

There was a farmer who was planting seeds in his field. Some seeds fell onto the hard path where the farmer walked. The birds saw these seeds. They flew down and ate all the seeds.

Some seeds fell beside the path. There were lots of rocks along the path. The little seeds fell in between the rocks, but there was very little soil there. The small plants sprouted and quickly began to grow by the rocks. When the hot sun came, the plants soon dried up. They needed deep soil to continue to grow. But their roots could not reach the water in the soil beneath the rocks.

Some seeds fell where there were weeds and thorns. These seeds grew into plants. But the weeds and thorns were stronger. They took all the water and blocked out the sunlight. The new plants could never grow strong.

Some of the seeds fell into the good dirt. Here they were safe from the birds. When the seeds sprouted, it was easy for their roots to push down into the soft dirt. Soon the seeds were strong young plants. Their stems reached up to the sunlight. Their roots pushed down to the water.

Before long, grain grew on the plants. The plants kept getting bigger and stronger. And as they grew, more grain grew on them. Each of these plants produced strong and healthy seeds. This was the end of Jesus' story.

The people who had listened to Jesus said, "Teacher, we do not understand this story. Can you explain it to us?"

Jesus answered their question. He said, "God's word is like the seeds. Some people hear God's word but do not take it into their hearts. They do not follow him. They are like the seeds eaten by the birds.

"Other people hear God's word and remember it for a little while. When they have problems, they forget about God. They do not ask God to protect them. These people are like the seeds growing among the rocks.

"There are other people who are like the seeds among the weeds and thorns. They put other things before their love for God. Soon there is no room for God in their lives and their belief in him goes away.

"But some people are like the seeds planted in the good soil. When God's love is planted in them, it begins to grow. Then they can share his love with others."

The Good Samaritan

Luke 10

Jesus spent much of his time on earth traveling from city to city telling people about God's love. One day a man asked Jesus, "What must a person do to get into heaven?"

Jesus replied, "What does God's word say?"

The man answered Jesus by saying, "The word of God says to love God with all your heart, all your strength, and all your mind. And you should love your neighbor as you love yourself."

Jesus told the man that what he said was true. If he followed those words he, too, would enter heaven. But the man still did not completely understand. So he asked, "Jesus, who is my neighbor?"

Jesus decided to answer this person by telling a story. At this time, the people in Jerusalem did not get along with the people from Samaria. They thought the Samaritans were bad people.

Jesus began his story. One day a man who was from Jerusalem was traveling down the road from Jerusalem to Jericho. As the man walked along, he was attacked by some robbers. The robbers jumped out from the bushes where they were hiding and hurt the man.

The robbers stole all his belongings. They even took some of his clothes. Then they left the hurt man on the side of the road.

Soon a priest from Jerusalem walked down the road. When he saw the hurt man lying there, he did not stop to help. He crossed to the other side of the road so he would be farther away from the man. The priest hurried along so he would not have to think about it anymore.

A little while later, another man was traveling down the same road. He, too, passed by the hurt man without stopping to help.

Finally a man from Samaria approached the hurt man. When he saw him, he felt sorry for him. It did not matter to him that they were not friends or that he did not know the man. The Samaritan only saw one thing. He saw someone who needed help.

The Samaritan went over to the hurt man. He cleaned the man's wounds. Then he bandaged them. He wrapped him in a warm blanket. Then the good Samaritan took the hurt man to a nearby inn. He paid the innkeeper for a room and watched over the hurt man all night. The next morning the Samaritan had to leave the inn. Before he left, he wanted to make sure the hurt man would have someone to take care of him.

He went to the innkeeper and gave him money. Then the Samaritan said, "Look after this man. When I return, I will give you more money for taking care of him."

The Samaritan did not know the hurt man. He showed great friendship for him by caring enough to stop and help someone he had never met before.

After Jesus finished telling the story, he asked, "Which one of the three men who saw the hurt man was the good neighbor?"

The man answered Jesus' question by saying, "The one who helped the hurt man."

Jesus said, "You must be a good Samaritan and help people who are in need."

Feeding the 5,000

Matthew 14, Mark 6, Luke 9

People from far and wide knew Jesus and his disciples. Crowds of people would ask Jesus to bless and heal them. And Jesus did. One day Jesus wanted to be alone with his disciples. He said to them, "We need to rest. Let us go to a quiet place." They got in a boat and moved away from shore.

Many people saw them leaving and began to run ahead of the boat. The people thought, "We will meet Jesus and his disciples when they get to the other side." Soon there were hundreds of people running to see Jesus.

As soon as Jesus and the disciples paddled the boat onto the shore, they were surrounded by a crowd.

Five thousand people came to see Jesus. Some of them had heard him speak in other towns. Many had seen him perform miracles. There were many sick and hurt people who had come to be healed by Jesus.

Some of the people had never seen Jesus. But they had heard stories about his miracles. And they wanted to see if what they heard was true.

Jesus saw how badly they needed him. He loved them all. Even though he was very tired, Jesus stayed until they were all healed. As he healed the people, he told them about God's love.

Jesus talked to the people for a long time. It began to get dark. "Jesus," the disciples said, "you must send these people home. It is late. Unless they go now, they will not reach their homes before dark. And we do not have food to give them."

But Jesus told the disciples, "Do not send these people away. Give them some food to eat."

"How can we feed all these people?" the disciples asked. "All we have is five loaves of bread and two small fish. This will not feed 5,000 people." The disciples were worried.

Jesus took the basket of food and said to the disciples, "Divide the people into smaller groups." Soon the people were sitting in small groups.

Jesus held the basket of food and prayed. "Thank you, God, for this food you have given to us," Jesus said.

After Jesus thanked God for the food, he broke the bread into pieces. "Share these pieces of bread and fish with the people," he said to the disciples.

Everyone ate as much as they wanted. Then Jesus said to the disciples, "Gather the extra food together." They did as Jesus instructed.

The disciples brought 12 baskets of leftover food to Jesus. Everyone knew that Jesus had performed a miracle because he started with only five loaves of bread and two small fish. Jesus had healed them, and then he fed them. Now the people truly believed that Jesus was the Son of God.

Jesus Walks on Water

Matthew 14

It was getting very late. Jesus and his disciples had been teaching all day. They were tired. "Row across the lake," he told the disciples. "The crowds will not be there. You can rest. I will come over later." The disciples got into the boat and began rowing across the lake.

Jesus was tired, too. He decided to go up on a hill by himself to pray. He wanted to spend time alone with God.

As it got darker, there was a storm. The wind began to blow. It blew harder and harder. It made big waves on the lake. The disciples' boat began to rock back and forth. They rowed faster, but it did not help. The wind just kept growing stronger. It pushed them away from the shore. They could not get to the other side of the lake.

Jesus saw them rowing, and he went to help them. Jesus walked out on the water toward their boat. The disciples saw someone approaching them, and they were frightened. "Who is it?" they asked. "Who could be walking on water in the middle of a storm?"

"Do not be afraid," Jesus said. "It is I." The disciples were very surprised. What was Jesus doing out there? Peter could not believe his eyes. He wanted to see if it was really Jesus.

"If it is really you, Jesus," Peter said, "tell me to walk on the water to you."

Jesus said, "Come to me, Peter."

Peter stepped out of the boat. He took one step, then another. He was walking on the water, too! Just as he was about to take another step, the wind blew very hard. Peter looked at the big waves and the storm. He was afraid. He began to sink. "Save me, Jesus," cried Peter.

Jesus reached out his hand. He pulled Peter up. "Peter, why were you afraid?" Jesus asked. "Did you think I might not help you?" Peter and Jesus got into the boat.

All of a sudden the wind quit blowing. The waves began to calm down. The boat stopped rocking. The disciples knew Jesus made the storm go away. They thanked him for saving them from the storm. "You are truly God's Son," they said. "Even the wind and the water obey you."

The Lost Sheep

Luke 15

Jesus cared about all people. Some of the people he cared about knew God. They prayed and worshiped him. They obeyed God's Law. Some even worked in the temple.

Jesus also cared about people who did not know God. He talked and ate with them. He visited with them in their homes. He shared stories with them.

This confused some of the men of the temple. One day Jesus heard these men talking. They said, "Why does Jesus spend time with people who do not know God?" To help the men understand, Jesus told this story.

Once there was a good shepherd. He spent every day watching over his flock of sheep. He had 100 sheep. Each morning he led them out into the pasture. There they had fresh green grass to eat. A clear, cool stream brought them water to drink. The good shepherd watched over them. All day the shepherd stayed with his flock. If any wild animals tried to hurt them, he protected his sheep.

Every evening, the shepherd led the flock back to the pen. As they entered the pen he counted them. This was to make sure that none of his sheep was lost.

One evening he counted 99 sheep. One was missing.

The good shepherd counted the sheep one more time. Ninety-nine of his sheep were safely in the pen. One was lost and needed him.

The good shepherd called for the lost sheep. It knew his voice. It might come to him. But it did not. The good shepherd walked back to the pasture. He looked around by the rocks where sometimes the sheep were caught. He looked in the bushes where he would find a stray sheep once in awhile. His lost sheep was not there. He walked  along the bank of the stream, calling for his little lost sheep. But it was not there either. The good shepherd kept looking. He did not give up.

When he found the lost sheep, the shepherd shouted with joy. He comforted the little sheep. Then he lifted it onto his shoulders and carried it back to the pen.

The good shepherd was very happy. He called all his neighbors together for a party. "Share my happiness," he said. "One of my sheep was lost, and I found it. It is safe." His friends were happy, too.

When Jesus finished telling this story, he said, "The same is true with all God's people. A person who gets lost from God and is found makes God very happy." Jesus wanted everyone to know and love God just as he did.

The men of the temple understood Jesus. God loves all people just like the good shepherd loves all his sheep.

The Prodigal Son

Luke 15

Forgiving others when they leave you is sometimes a hard thing to do. But Jesus wanted everyone to know that God loves them, even when what they do makes other people sad. Jesus told this story to a crowd of people so they would learn how important it is to understand God's love and to forgive others.

Jesus' story began with a man who had two sons. The older son did his chores and tried to be good. The younger son wanted to travel and see the world.

The younger son asked his father to give him the money that he was saving for him. The father was very upset that his younger son wanted to leave home. The father wanted to protect his son, but he decided to give him the money anyway. This made the younger son very happy. He packed his things and set off to see the world.

He thought about the wonderful things he could buy with the money that his father had given him. The younger son began his new life. He lived like a king. He spent money freely. He bought only the best clothes and ate only the finest food.

It did not take long before all of his money was gone. He had to sell his expensive clothes. Soon he had nothing left. He did not even have enough money to buy a single piece of bread.

He had no money, no friends, and nowhere to live. He was far away from his family. He felt all alone. There was no one to help him.

He tried to find a job. But the only job he could find was feeding pigs. He was so hungry that he found himself wishing he could at least have some of the food the pigs were eating.

As he sat there watching the pigs eat, the younger son thought about his father and brother. He also thought about his life back home. He always had plenty of food to eat there. Even the people who worked for his father had plenty of food and a warm place to stay. He began to cry. He wanted things to be the way they were before he left home. He was very sad and unhappy.

He wondered if his father would let him work in the fields. If his father gave him a job as a helper, he would have plenty of food to eat, and he would have a safe place to sleep.

The younger son knew that he had acted selfishly, so he decided to return home to see if his father would give him a job.

The younger son began his trip home. While he was still a very long way off, his father saw him. When he saw his son, his heart filled with joy. He ran to meet him. The father threw his arms around his younger son, kissed him, and cried tears of joy. The son said, "Father, I was wrong to leave you. I should not be called your son. Can you please forgive me and let me work for you?"

The father turned to one of his workers and said, "Quick. Bring a new robe, and put it on him. We shall have a huge feast to celebrate my son returning home. For I thought he was lost forever, and now he is safe here with me."

Meanwhile the older son had been working hard in the fields. He decided to take a break. As he walked closer to the house, he heard happy music and dancing. He smelled food cooking. Then he saw the big celebration at the house. The older son was quite puzzled by all these things and wondered what was going on.

He called to one of the workers, "What is happening? Why is my father having this big party?"

The worker said, "Your younger brother has returned home. Your father has thrown a party to celebrate."

The older brother was angry. He refused to go in the house. His father came outside and asked him to join the celebration. He wanted his two sons to be together again.

The older son said, "No. I will not welcome him back. He left me here to run the farm. He took your money and ran off to the city. He spent all the money on clothes and food. Now, when all the money is gone, you welcome him back as if nothing happened. You give him a party for not working, but you did not throw a party for me."

The father looked at his older child and said, "My son, please try to understand. You have always been safe here with me. Everything I have is yours. But your brother, who I thought was lost, is alive. We must celebrate his return."

Jesus told this story so the people would understand how important it is to love and forgive others.

Jesus and the Children

Matthew 19

Jesus liked to answer questions from those who came to hear him speak. The people would try to understand what he was teaching. Wise men were very interested in what he had to say.

Jesus spent much of his time talking about God and healing the sick. Wherever they would go, Jesus and his disciples were very often surrounded by large groups of people. Even as they walked from one place to another, people would follow them. Sometimes they had to clear a path just to get through the big crowds of people that had come to see Jesus.

People often brought their babies and young children to see Jesus. They wanted him to bless them. They were trying to be good parents. They were trying to obey God's rules. The children were excited, too. They wanted to see Jesus. They wanted to be near him and touch him.

One day the disciples saw the children running toward them. The children wanted to see Jesus. The disciples thought that Jesus was too busy to see the children. They tried to stop them from seeing Jesus.

The disciples said, "Jesus has more important things to do than to see children." They told the parents and children they could not talk to Jesus. They asked them to go away.

When Jesus found out what the disciples had said and done, he was not happy. He went to the disciples and told them that he wanted to see the children.

"Do not stop the children from coming to me," Jesus told his disciples. Jesus knew that children were special. He knew it was important for them to see him and hear him speak.

"Let the little children come to me. The kingdom of God belongs to hearts like these," said Jesus. The children came to Jesus. He took them in his arms. He wanted them to know that he was not too busy for them. Jesus blessed the children and told them he loved them.

Zaccaeus

Luke 19

Zacchaeus was a wealthy man. He lived in the city of Jericho. He worked as a tax collector. Jericho was a very busy city. Many people came to sell all kinds of handmade pottery, clothing, and food. Each time they sold something, they had to pay tax money to Zacchaeus.

Many people who wanted to worship God passed by the market area on their way to the temple. If they bought anything, Zacchaeus would collect money from them, too.

Zacchaeus collected more money than what was owed. He would keep the extra money for himself. The people knew he took too much money, and they did not like him.

One day Jesus and his disciples came to Jericho. When the people heard he was coming, they lined up along the streets to see him. They wanted to hear him teach.

Zacchaeus heard that Jesus was on his way to Jericho. He had heard stories about Jesus. Zacchaeus decided to go see him. "I should be able to see Jesus as he walks by," he thought. But there was one problem. Zacchaeus was very short. All the other people were already lined up along the road. Zacchaeus tried to look over their shoulders, but he could not see anything. The crowd was too big and too tall.

Zacchaeus thought to himself, "There must be something I can do." He looked around for something that would make him taller. Suddenly he started to run. He ran past the crowd and got ahead of where Jesus was walking. He saw a big, tall sycamore tree. "If I climb high up in the tree," thought Zacchaeus, "I will be able to see Jesus even when the crowd surrounds him." He climbed high in the tree and waited for Jesus.

The crowd began to cheer. The people's voices became louder and louder. He knew that Jesus was coming closer. He could hardly wait. Soon Jesus would be walking under the branch where Zacchaeus was sitting. Now he was sure he would get to see Jesus.

From his branch, Zacchaeus watched for Jesus. "There he is!" Zacchaeus said to himself. "There is Jesus."

Zacchaeus watched as Jesus moved closer. The crowd was all around Jesus. They were almost directly below him. Then, just as Jesus walked underneath the sycamore tree, he stopped. Jesus looked straight up at Zacchaeus. Everyone stopped. Then Jesus said, "Zacchaeus, come down here. I am going to your house."

Zacchaeus was very surprised. Jesus was coming to his house. What did that mean? He thought to himself, "Why does Jesus want to come to my house?" He climbed down from the tree as fast as he could. Then he ran to his house and got ready for Jesus.

The crowd did not understand. "Why is Jesus going to Zacchaeus' house? He takes more money from us than he should, and he is a bad man," the people said. "Zacchaeus does not obey God's law."

But Jesus did go to Zacchaeus' house. While they were together, Zacchaeus told Jesus he was sorry for all the things he had done wrong. "Jesus, I will give half of what I have to the poor," said Zacchaeus. "And I will give back four times more than I took from the people I overcharged."

This made Jesus very happy. He said, "Zacchaeus, I have come so people will know God. Today God is with you."

The Last Supper

Matthew 26

Jesus and his disciples were busy preparing for a wonderful celebration called the Passover. Passover is a time when people remember and worship God for saving them from slavery.

Jesus taught in the temple every day. All the people loved to hear him speak. But the temple leaders did not want Jesus there. They were afraid too many people were following his teachings. They were also afraid the people would want Jesus to be their leader. They became jealous and decided they needed a plan to get rid of him.

One of the 12 disciples that traveled with Jesus was named Judas. It was his job to take care of the money for the disciples. Sometimes he wanted to take some of the money for himself. He had heard that the temple leaders wanted to get rid of Jesus. So Judas met with the leaders. He asked, "What will you be willing to give me if I hand over Jesus to you?"

The leaders offered Judas money. They told him they would give him 30 pieces of silver if he helped them with their plan. Judas was greedy, and he took their money.

Meanwhile Jesus had sent Peter and John to prepare a room for the Passover meal. Before the two left, Jesus told them that a man carrying a jar of water would meet them as they entered the city. Peter and John were to follow the man to his house. Then they were to say, "Do you have a room where we can serve our Passover meal?"

Jesus said that the man would show them to the room. Peter and John did as they were told. They found the man with the jar, and he showed them to the room.

Later Jesus and all 12 disciples gathered together in the room to celebrate Passover. Jesus told them how to prepare the meal. The disciples did everything just as Jesus said. They had plenty of bread and wine for everyone.

Before the meal was served, Jesus brought out a bowl of water. He used the water to wash his disciples' feet.

Jesus told the disciples that the time would soon come when his life on earth would be over. When the disciples heard him say these things, they were sad. They had been with Jesus for a long time, and he was their friend. While they were eating the Passover meal, Jesus looked at them and said, "One of you will betray me."

Each of the disciples came to Jesus and said, "Surely, it is not I, is it?" They could not believe that anyone would betray Jesus.

"The one I give this bread to will be the one who betrays me," whispered Jesus to John.

Then Jesus broke off a piece of bread and handed it to Judas. Jesus knew Judas was a greedy man. He also knew that Judas had agreed to turn him over to the leaders for 30 pieces of silver. "Go," Jesus said to Judas, "and do what you have planned." Judas left the room where they were eating the Passover meal and went to talk to the leaders.

Then Jesus did something very special. He took a cup of wine and some bread. He blessed it and said, "You will remember me whenever you eat this bread and drink this wine." Although the disciples did not understand what he meant, they did as Jesus said. Jesus knew many things were about to happen. He knew that the disciples would need to be strong and remember all the lessons he had taught them. Then Jesus and his disciples sang songs to praise God.

Jesus told the disciples he would have to leave them soon. The disciples did not know what the temple leaders had planned, but Jesus knew. He said, "Do not be afraid of what will happen. You must remember to love one another as I have loved you."

Jesus Is Alive

Matthew 26–28

After the last supper, Jesus and his disciples went to a garden to pray. He asked his disciples to stay awake and keep watch. Then Jesus found a quiet corner of the garden where he could be alone to pray. While Jesus prayed his disciples fell asleep.

Jesus knew many sad things were about to happen. He also knew the disciples would have to remain strong. They would need to remember all the lessons he had taught them. So Jesus prayed, "Father, I want people to know you and your love as I do. I have taught them about you and your ways. I know what you have planned for me."

After Jesus finished praying, he woke up the disciples. "Why are you sleeping? Please stay awake," he said.

Jesus saw Judas walking towards him. He was with a group of soldiers. Then Judas whispered to the soldiers, "The one I kiss will be Jesus. He is the one you want."

Judas began walking toward Jesus. He was surprised when Jesus asked, "Are you betraying me with a kiss?" Jesus already knew Judas would betray him.

When the disciples saw what was happening they tried to fight the soldiers. But Jesus told them, "Do not fight."

The soldiers grabbed Jesus, and the disciples ran away. The soldiers brought Jesus in front of an angry group of temple leaders. The leaders wanted to get rid of him. "Jesus must die," the leaders said, "because he says he is the Son of God."

The temple leaders hung Jesus on a cross to die. Jesus' friends came to be near him. They were very sad. They did not understand God's plan.

After Jesus died a good man named Joseph took Jesus' body. Joseph lovingly wrapped the body in a clean linen cloth. He then placed Jesus in a small cave called a tomb. The tomb was cut from rock.

Everyone watched as the body of Jesus was placed in the tomb. A stone was rolled in front to cover the mouth of the tomb. The angry temple leaders made some guards stand in front of the tomb to keep watch.

Three days had passed since Jesus' body was placed in the tomb. Everyone was very sad but not for long. Something unusual happened. An earthquake rumbled and shook the ground. The noise was very loud! The ground shook so hard that the guards fell over.

They were frightened as they saw an angel appear. The angel rolled back the stone from the mouth of the tomb. The guards were so frightened that they ran away. Jesus' body was not in the tomb.

Mary Magdalene was one of Jesus' friends. She was on her way to visit the tomb. When Mary saw the stone had been rolled away, she ran inside to look for Jesus. "Where is Jesus? What has happened to him?" she cried.

Mary saw a stranger sitting inside the tomb. It was an angel. "Do not be afraid," the angel said. "I know you are looking for Jesus. But he is not here. He is alive. You must tell the disciples that Jesus is alive!"

Jesus had told Mary that he would rise on the third day. She ran to find the disciples to tell them the good news!

Peter

John 21

The disciples heard about the angel from Mary. They were happy for her. But where was Jesus? Was he really alive? Peter wanted to see Jesus, too. "What should we do?" asked Peter.

The disciples decided to go to the Sea of Galilee. It was almost dark when they arrived, and they had not eaten. "We are all hungry," said Peter. "Let us go fishing so we can catch some fish to eat." So they went fishing. They rowed their boat out from the shore and took out their net.

They put their net in the water and waited. But when they checked the net, there were no fish. The net was still empty. They lowered the net back in the water. When they checked the net later, there were still no fish.

They stayed out on the water all night, but they did not catch a single fish. Suddenly they heard a voice calling to them. The voice said, "Have you caught any fish?"

"No, we have not," answered Peter, "and we have been here all night."

"Cast your net out on the other side of the boat. That is where the fish are," said the man on shore. The disciples did not think moving the net would help. But they did as the man said. In just a minute or two, their net was full of fish. It was so heavy they could not even lift it.

The disciples were surprised. They had been fishing all night long, and had not caught a single fish. Now their net was so full they could not even lift it into the boat. They asked, "Who is this man?" Then one of the disciples said, "It is Jesus! The man on the shore is Jesus!"

Peter looked up. He was so happy. It was Jesus! Peter could not wait for the nets to be pulled into the boat. He wanted to be with Jesus. He dove into the water and swam as fast as he could. When Peter reached Jesus he had a big smile on his face. The other disciples pulled the net in and rowed back to shore. Jesus had built a fire, and he was cooking breakfast. They were all happy to see him again. Jesus was alive, and he was God's Son.

While they were eating their breakfast, Jesus asked, "Peter, do you love me?"

"Yes, Jesus, you know I do," Peter answered.

"Feed my sheep," said Jesus. A few minutes later, Jesus asked him again, "Peter, do you love me?"

Peter looked at Jesus and said, "Yes."

Jesus replied, "Feed my sheep." Then a third time Jesus asked Peter, "Do you love me?"

Peter was very sad that Jesus kept asking him the same question. He said, "Jesus, you know everything. Certainly you know that I love you." But Jesus would soon go to heaven. He wanted Peter to know how much he loved him.

"I want you to take care of my followers," said Jesus. Peter did what Jesus asked. He spent his life helping other people and teaching them about God.

Jesus Goes to Heaven

Matthew 28; Acts 1 & 2

Jesus knew his disciples still needed him. He wanted them to believe in him. They must remember the things he had taught them about heaven and God's kingdom, so Jesus appeared to 11 of his disciples as they were eating.

Jesus said to them, "You must remember all the things I have taught you. I want you to teach them to others. They must obey God's rules. And you must teach people to love one another as they love themselves. Do not forget me and the things I have taught you." Then Jesus said, "Remember I will be with you always."

Jesus led his disciples to a place called Bethany. They had many questions for him, because they still did not understand God's plan for them. Jesus said they were to stay in Jerusalem until they received a special gift from God. "Once you have received this special gift, you will tell everyone about me and about God's love for them," he said.

Jesus lifted up his hands and gave them a blessing. As the disciples watched, Jesus went up into a cloud. He was gone! The disciples kept watching for Jesus. They waited and waited for him to come back.

Where had he gone? The disciples wondered if Jesus had gone to heaven. He had told them his work on earth was finished.

The disciples stood looking up where they had last seen Jesus. Suddenly two men wearing white robes stood beside them.

The men said, "Why are you still standing here looking at the sky? Jesus has gone to heaven. One day he will come back the same way he left."

The disciples said a prayer to God. Then they returned to Jerusalem just as Jesus had told them. There they gave thanks for all that they had seen and heard.

Jesus and the disciples had been together for several years. He had been teaching the word of God to them. The disciples had seen Jesus perform many miracles. They had seen sick people get better. They had seen hungry people given food to eat. And they had felt God's love when they were with him.

The disciples also learned about heaven. Jesus had told them what a wonderful place God had prepared for those who believed in him.

Jesus had given them a very important job. They were responsible for sharing God's love with everyone.

Jesus had told the disciples to stay in Jerusalem until God sent a special gift. The disciples gathered for a holiday called the Pentecost. People would come to Jersualem from all over the world to celebrate this holiday.

The disciples were gathered together in one place to pray to God. Suddenly a loud sound came from heaven. It sounded like a strong rushing wind. Everyone in Jerusalem heard the wind and came to see what happened.

Suddenly fire appeared on the disciples. This was the spirit of God. This was the special gift Jesus told them to expect. When the disciples spoke, every person heard in his own language what they were saying.

When the people saw and heard the disciples speaking in different languages, they were confused. But Peter stood up and said, "People listen to me. A long time ago God said that the day would come when this would happen. This is God's promise to us. It is God's special gift."

Peter kept talking about God's love and the kingdom of God. The people listened to what he had to say. Many of them were very sad because they knew they had done wrong. Peter told them to open their hearts to God's love. Thousands of people listened to the words Peter said. Everyone was happy. They listened, and they learned how to share God's love.

Saul

Acts 9 & 16

There was a bad man named Saul. He did not believe in Jesus. He wanted to put anyone who followed Jesus into jail. Saul and some of his friends decided to travel to the city of Damascus. He knew a man there who would help them find people who followed Jesus.

Saul wanted to take these people as prisoners to Jerusalem. Many of the people were afraid of Saul. They did not like the way he treated them.

Jesus knew what Saul was doing to his followers. He did not want Saul to hurt his people anymore. Saul and his friends approached Damascus. When they were almost there, Saul was surrounded by a bright light. The light was so bright that he fell to the ground and tried to shield his eyes. Then he heard a voice say, "Saul, why are you doing this to me?"

Saul was afraid. He trembled as he asked, "Who are you?"

"I am Jesus, the one you do not believe or trust," said Jesus. "Go into the city. There you will be told what you must do."

The men traveling with Saul heard the voice of Jesus, but they did not see him. Saul stood up and tried to open his eyes. He could not see. His friends led him into Damascus. For three days Saul was blind. He would not eat or drink.

Jesus told one of his disciples to find Saul. He wanted the disciple to help Saul see again.

Jesus' disciple said, "I have heard of this man. He is very mean. He wants to put people in jail who follow your teachings."

But Jesus said, "You must do as I say. I have great plans for Saul." The disciple did as he was told.

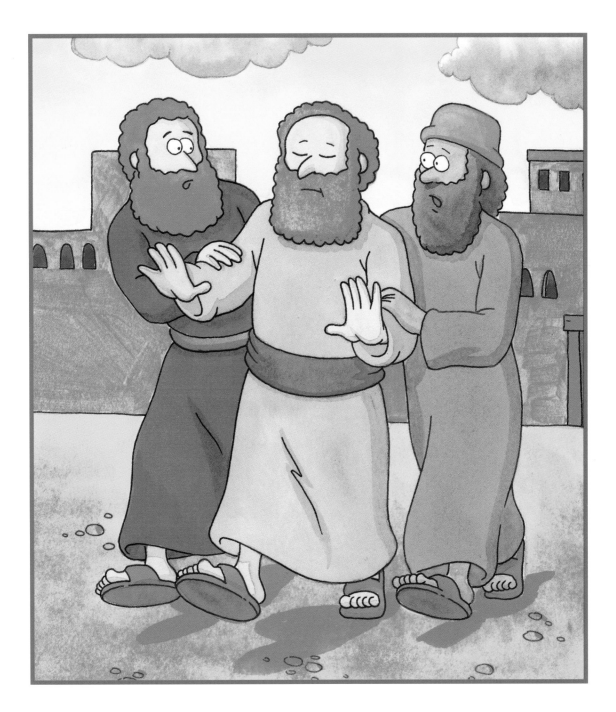

The disciple went to the house where Saul was staying. He put his hands on Saul's eyes and said, "Jesus sent me here to help you. You will see again." When he removed his hands, Saul could see. He was baptized and filled with God's spirit.

Saul was now going to teach people about God. He wanted to show everyone that he had changed. He even changed his name. Now people would call him Paul. Paul would be a very special helper for God's people. He went from place to place telling people about God.

Some people were still afraid of Paul. But eventually they realized that he was now working for God. There were people, however, who did not like the new Paul. They were upset at how he had changed. They wanted to hurt him. Paul became friends with another man who believed in God. His name was Silas. The two traveled far and wide. They told everyone they met about Jesus and his love.

In one town where Paul and Silas were teaching, some of the people did not like them. These people had Paul and Silas thrown into jail.

Paul and Silas were not worried. They knew God was with them and would protect them. They sang songs and prayed. Other prisoners heard them singing and praying. Suddenly an earthquake shook the prison. The jail doors flew open. The chains that held everyone's hands and feet came open. The earthquake woke up the jailer. He ran into the jail. He was afraid the prisoners had run away.

But God had a different plan. When the jailer got to the jail and looked inside the cells, he heard Paul's voice. Paul said, "Do not worry. We are all here."

The jailer could not believe his eyes. He fell down in front of Paul and Silas and said, "What can I do to show my love for God?" Paul and Silas knew what to say. They told the man to believe in Jesus. The jailer and his whole family believed in Jesus, too. The next day the jailer received orders to let Paul and Silas go free.

Paul and Silas continued to teach people about God.

Jesus Will Come Again

Revelation 1–22

John was one of Jesus' closest followers and friends. After Jesus went to heaven, John traveled many places teaching people about Jesus. Some leaders did not like John. They did not want him to teach about Jesus. They decided to send him away to an island. Then John would not be able to tell people about Jesus.

One day while John was praying, he heard a loud voice behind him. The voice sounded like a trumpet. The voice said, "I am going to show you things that will happen in the future. I want you to write down what I show you. Then you can share these things with other people."

John turned around and saw someone. It looked like Jesus. His face was shining brightly, like the sun. He wore a white robe and a sash of gold. His voice sounded like rushing waters. John was surprised at what he saw. The voice said, "I am Jesus. I was dead, but now I am alive and I will live forever."

Again, Jesus told him, "I am here to share with you things that no one else knows. You must write these things down and tell others."

John saw many things that day. He saw an open door to heaven. Through the open door, he saw God's throne. There was a rainbow around the throne. The throne was surrounded by winged creatures who sang all day and all night. They sang, "Holy, holy, holy is the Lord God Almighty, who was and is to come."

John saw and heard many other things. He heard a loud voice say, "I am making everything new. There will be a new heaven and a new earth. I will wipe the tears from your eyes. There will be no more dying and no more pain. To all those who are thirsty, I will give them the water of life. I am coming soon. I will bring your rewards with me. And I will give these rewards to everyone according to what they have done."

John wrote down what he saw and heard.

Then Jesus said, "Yes, I am coming soon."